AKNOWLEDGEMENT

Contents

Acknowledgements

- The problem which Indian society still suffers is cruelty against women is based on dowry; domestic violence against women in India has its root at the demand of dowry. Dowry may happen in any families there's no difference between rich, bourgeoisie, poor, educated or uneducated. When a marriage is fixed no one is worry as to how clever, intellectual, and homely the girl is, but all that matters is, how much money and luxuries will she get to husband's home. With the passage of time dowry became a customary part in Indian society and became demanding dowry as their right in order to marry a woman, and gradually the dowry became violence to women when the groom's family didn't get enough dowry, leading to harassment or cruelty of brides and also dowry deaths, especially in certain parts of India. Dowry demands affect the lives of females socially, economically and culturally.

1. The custom of dowry in Indian marriages is a deep-seated cultural phenomenon that has been described as one of the largest obstacles to "confront India on her road to economic and social justice Indeed, one of India's greatest social failures is the extraordinarily high level of gender inequality and female deprivation that has persisted in the nation for the last several decades through cultural practices such as dowry. The custom is held responsible for a number of problems perpetrated against the nation's women, including dowry violence, bride burning, and wife murder. Although unanimously regarded by legislators and scholars as a perpetrator of social detriment against women, the Dowry Prohibition Act of 1961 that outlawed the practice has been remarkably unsuccessful in reducing the frequency of its occurrence. In fact, not only has the demand for dowry not been eliminated, it has become increasingly popular among the upper echelons of the Hindu society where it originated and has become widespread even among various communities of Muslims, Christians, and tribal groups all across India The failure of legislation to eliminate the payment of dowry in Indian marriages likely stems from a fundamental misunderstanding of both the effects and more importantly, the causes of the practice. I argue that dowries exist because of a

combination of two reasons. First, there is an excess supply of women in the Indian marriage market that results in the use of dowry as an equilibrating mechanism. Secondly, a differential in the patterns of human capital accumulation of men and women have led to a larger positive benefit from marriage for women than for men, the net difference of which is theoretically equivalent to the amount of the dowry. Both these explanations for the existence of dowry are fundamentally grounded in the powerful social and cultural ideologies of marriage held by the vast majority of Indian society. Furthermore, the phenomena of dowry-related violence and female infanticide, which are the cause of substantial detriment to the social welfare of Indian women, are intimately linked with and probably symptomatic of the dowry tradition. Legal and other strategies must be used to eliminate both the root causes of the dowry tradition as well as address its grave outward symptoms. Definition of Dowry Historically, dowry has been an integral and institutionalized aspect of traditional arranged Hindu marriage. Over hundreds of years, however, the definition of the term has evolved from the ceremonial and voluntary gift giving of the bride's family to a form of monetary extortion demanded by the groom's family. Studies on the origins of the tradition postulate that dowry originally and ideally denoted gifts of kayadanda, such as ornaments, expensive clothes and other precious items referenced in ancient texts on marriage ritual, voluntarily presented to both the bride and groom's families during the time of marriage Moreover, the practice was derived from the high cultural and spiritual merit accorded to gift givers and gift giving in the Vedas and other Hindu literature.

As such, dowry was originally used as a means to both sanctify material wealth and also enhance social status in marriage. The modern phenomenon of dowry, however, reflects a change in the system such that the presentation of gifts no longer remains a voluntary process. Presently in India, bride's families are often compelled to provide dowry in the name of gift giving. Evaluated in terms of total cash value, the amount of the dowry is negotiated by the groom's family based on their social and economic status. The higher the socioeconomic status of the groom's family, the higher the dowry demanded the exact negotiation for dowry is often done through a mediator so that the marriage retains some semblance of sanctity and does not appear to be an entirely monetary transaction. The modern practice of dowry, therefore, is characterized by a shift from voluntary to forced gift giving, as well as the primary role of the groom's family in determining the demand for gifts from the bride's family. In the way it is currently understood, the term dowry is a broad reference to the totality of assets transferred from the bride's family to the groom's at the time of a marriage. The total transfer can be broken down into three basic parts. Firstly, there are the property transfers to the bride, which according to Indian law should legally be under her name and control. Second, there are those gifts that continue to be part of the ceremonial aspect of the marriage and symbolize union between the two families. Ideally, these would be matched by reciprocal gifts of equal value from the groom's family. Finally, there are those assets that can be called "marriage payments" and are given "with the explicit understanding that without them the marriage contract will be voided (Sen 78)." In an economic analysis, it is this final aspect that constitutes the actual significant economic cost of dowry for a bride's family, and is perhaps the most costly among the three aspects of the dowry. The Marriage Market the economic underpinnings and causes of dowry can only be fully understood within the framework of economic theory on marriage. Established economic views the market for marriage as one in which people bargain for a spouse who maximizes their utility gains from marriage (Becker). Traditional Indian Hindu marriages can operate within this framework, but with one clear distinction—these marriages are almost always arranged by the families of the prospective spouses. Families search the marriage market for suitable matches, examining quantifiable characteristics such as age, caste, socioeconomic background, labor market earnings for men, and household labor skills (such as cooking, cleaning, and childbearing) for women. Eventually, it is the family, and not just the individual, which makes the final decision as to whether or not the marriage will take place. The concept of arranged marriage does to some extent confound the fundamental economic principles of individual choice in marriage, but for simplicity's sake, the assumption is made that there is a single utility function for both the individual and his or her family. Customs of Indian Marriage Societal and religious dictates have had a profound effect on Indian Hindu marital conventions. As already mentioned, the marriages are normally arranged by the families of the prospective spouses. This phenomenon essentially precludes any potential "love" marriages, as these marriages are looked down upon by the community, especially if the bride and groom are not of comparable caste and socioeconomic status. Other marital codes are particularly strict for women. Most Indian communities impose an unofficial age limit by which time young women must be married. Although the age varies somewhat from region to region, families that fail to marry off their daughters by such a time are subject to the gravest censure and shame. Beyond the immediate consequence where the family will be forced to financially support an unmarried daughter for the rest of her life, the social condemnation that accompanies such a situation also carries with it the weight of economic penalization. Often, the offending family will lose employees, customers, and general goodwill in the market implication of traditional Indian custom is that a daughter, once married, belongs to and must live with her husband's family. Any labor market earnings and household skills of the bride become the assets of the husband's family, and any sustenance costs become their liability. Furthermore, as per the tradition of Indian families, all assets (such as wages or dowry) and all liabilities (sustenance costs such as food, clothing, and shelter) of the bride are pooled with those of other members of the family. The parents-in-law then make the final decisions about how the income should be spent or saved As such, in the traditional Indian household, individual rights become subsidiary to those of the family-in-law. These three aspects of the traditions of Indian marriage—the social mandate requiring women to be married by a young age, the transfer of all financial assets and liabilities of a bride to the groom's family, and the household pooling of resources—constitute the dominant cultural, social, and ideological forces that have led to the existence and persistence of dowry in Indian society. Causes of Dowry Economic theory, which views the market for marriage as one in which people bargain for a spouse who maximizes their utility gains from marriage, when combined with the realities of various sociological factors, presents an interesting perspective on the reasons behind the existence of the dowry system in India. Under the assumption of a perfectly competitive marriage market with perfect information, the existence of a dowry can be seen as the combined result of a few different forces. The "Marriage Squeeze" and Excess Supply of Wives Theoretical work by economists on marriage transactions has stipulated that dowries are likely to occur when equilibrium conditions result in an excess supply of women who want to marry and enter the marriage market .An excess supply of women, or a relative scarcity of men in the marriage market, can be equilibrated through the use of the marital cost of dowry. In theory, the monetary cost of the dowry increases as the supply of women wanting to marry rises, shifting the supply curve enough to balance the demand for wives. Some scholars have argued that the excess supply argument is suspect for the case of Indian society because the nation's gender-ratio imbalance is notoriously tilted towards fewer women than men, rather than reverse (Sen 80). In fact, the country's female-male ratio has declined from 972 women per thousand men in 1901 to less than 927 women per thousand men in 1991 However, there is a fundamental flaw in examining the total gender ratio as an indicator of the relative supply of women in the marriage market, for certain social customs of Indian society cause distinct peculiarities in the way the Indian marriage market is divided between men and women. In India, Hindu marriages are based on social and religious beliefs that allow men to marry at virtually any age, while women are required to marry by a much younger age. Although the maximum age limit for marriage varies for women in different regions of India, the central belief is that a daughter who remains unmarried after the socially determined age will thereafter be ineligible for marriage, and as such, will bring to her family social disgrace, the financial liability of her sustenance, and certain types of economic sanctions imposed by the rest of the community. The most significant implication of such an ideology is that the Indian marriage market becomes divided into an older male cohort and a much younger female cohort. Thus, the actual gender ratio in the Indian marriage market cannot be detected in the nation's total gender ratio or even in same age group or same time period gender ratios. Instead, it is the relative numbers of the younger female cohort as compared with the older male cohort that determines the true ratio of eligible men and women who want to marry. This peculiar gender division leads to some key insight about the rising costs of dowry, for the structure of India's marriage market is highly affected by one of the nation's greatest obstacles to social and economic progress: population growth. Recent empirical work has shown that India's surge in population growth over the last several decades has led to a "marriage squeeze theory, a "marriage squeeze" means that a population with a declining mortality rate and increasing birth rate will have larger younger cohorts than older ones. Because women tend to marry older men in Indian society, the eligible women in India's marriage market would therefore belong to a younger and hence larger cohort. Essentially, a high population growth would lead to a gender ratio in the marriage market characterized by a surplus of women, and the amount of this surplus would depend on the actual rate of population growth. A "marriage squeeze," therefore, by causing an increase in the supply of women in the marriage market, would also cause an upward shift in the amount of dowry needed to equilibrate that market. 8 in one region of southern India, data and research estimate that the marriage squeeze ratio has caused a "significant increase in net real dowry transfers over time In considering this trend as a result of the surplus of women in the marriage market, it is also important to note that the area studied was a region in which female mortality at younger ages exceeds male mortality. In fact, the gender ratio in the region has tilted towards more men than women in the total population ever since the turn of the century. The surplus of women over men at marriageable ages, therefore, indicates that the population growth was large enough to outweigh the fact there have always been more women than men within the same age cohort. India's alarmingly high population growth led to a subsequent increase in the size of the younger female cohort in the marriage market, thereby inducing a "marriage squeeze" that can be held at least partly responsible for the existence of as well as the recent increase in costs of dowries. Divergent Patterns of Human Capital Accumulation The theory of the "marriage squeeze," based on the Indian social phenomenon where younger women tend to marry older men, uses India's high population growth of the last several decades to explain the increase in the average cost of dowries. However, the other prevalent customs and attitudes of Indian marriage are another extremely significant aspect of the economic rationale for why the practice of dowry persists in Indian society. Aside from the excess supply of women in the marriage market already discussed, the existence of dowry may alternatively be attributed to an inherent differential between the gains from marriage for men and women. This explanation has one very important implication: the benefits of marriage for women exceed the benefits gained from marriage by men. It is thus the net difference between these marital gains that the groom's family appropriates as dowry, or "marriage payment." The discrepancy in marital gains can be seen as having two components. Firstly, traditional social norms inhibit the acquisition of market-oriented human capital by women and instead p30romote procurement of household-oriented human capital, which in turn can only be fully utilized within the context of marriage. Secondly, individual and family utility, which in economic theory is generally defined as "well-being" or "happiness," is derived not only from the consumption of material goods, but also from a desire to uphold a good name and reputation in a community by adhering to its prevalent social and cultural beliefs. Neoclassical economic theory fails to take into account the utility derived from social acceptance, but it is only by understanding the social and ideological forces of Indian society that it becomes possible to fully understand the economic and market forces that have led to the existence of dowry. In this context, two broad categories of human capital can be defined: market specific human capital, which contributes to productivity and earnings potential in the labor market, and household specific human capital, which contributes to productivity and skills that increase the social status of the household and family, Capital accumulation decisions are made during childhood by parents and families. It is assumed that market specific human capital generally requires monetary investment, and is obtained through formal education and training, while household specific capital can generally be acquired without any monetary investment through training and work in the household under the supervision of a senior female member of the household. It is reasonable to assume that families consider several factors when making decisions about human capital investment for their children. These include the utility derived from their children's preferences, the family utility derived from adhering to social customs regarding the appropriate forms of capital accumulation for different genders, and finally, the expected rate of return on the family's monetary investment into children's market specific human capital. In this context, three prevalent features of Indian society will be discussed in their relevance to decisions regarding the acquisition of human capital for women. Perhaps the most basic phenomenon of Indian marriage is that a daughter, once married, essentially becomes the property of her husband's family. All assets, including any labor market earnings, household skills, and dowry, are transferred to the family-in-law. Sons, however, are almost always the source of future income and dependence for parents during their old age. As such, money invested into the acquisition of market specific human capital for a son is usually regarded as a form of investment into parents' future consumption. Monetary investment into a daughter's acquisition of human capital, however, returns no specific financial yield, although there may be benefits accrued due to any utility parents may derive from the happiness of their children. Such financial circumstances help explain the widespread decision of Indian households to allocate most or all resources intended for children's consumption to the investment of market specific human capital for sons, while daughters are generally forced to invest in the zero cost acquisition of household specific human capital .The investment decisions made by Indian families regarding the acquisition of human capital for their children are likely to be influenced by the large differential in labor market earnings between men and women. Many studies have determined that there is an enormous amount of wage discrimination in the Indian labor market In particular, research has shown that Indian women with post-secondary schooling earn about 21% less than Indian men, and that about 67-77% of this wage gap may be attributed to discrimination. The primary significance of this wage discrepancy in decisions of human capital acquisition is that investment into market specific human capital for daughters yields a much lower expected real rate of return than such investment for sons. The wage discrepancy in the labor market is another reason that Indian parents tend to invest less in market specific human capital for their daughters, as they realize that the yield from such an investment in terms of labor market earnings would be relatively meager In addition to rationally and economically analyzing the expected return on investment, Indian families are also heavily influenced by the strong social and cultural beliefs that view the acquisition of economic resources by women with intense antagonism. Indian social structural ideologies have long regarded women as the stable foundation of the family. Appropriate responsibilities for women have generally been limited to household tasks such as childbearing, cooking, cleaning, and other social and religious activities such as singing for community events or planning religious ceremonies known as pujas. Moreover, excessive education or "education of the wrong kind, such as education that grants her the means of economic self-sufficiency, increases the probability that a girl will gain an unseemly amount of independence, violate her traditional role and disrupt familial and societal harmony in the future Depending on a family's adherence to such prevailing social attitudes, daughters are for yet another generally restricted to developing only household oriented skills, while sons are allocated the funding needed to gain market skills through school, college, and job training. Thus, due to a variety of both economic and social reasons, women in Indian societies are raised with a much higher proportion of household specific human capital relative to market specific human capital. The most significant implication of the discrepancy in patterns of human capital accumulation for men and women is on the relative benefits they receive in marriage. The most fundamental characteristic of household specific human capital is that it can be fully utilized only within the married state. For example, the benefits of skills such as those specific to bearing and raising children become irrelevant out of marriage, for out-of-wedlock and divorced motherhood are considered among the greatest social disgraces for Indian women, often provoking severe censure and disdain by the community at large. Consequently, women who have acquired large amounts of household specific human capital stand to receive two major benefits from marriage. First, there is an increase in consumption and utility derived from a society that regards marriage in high esteem. And secondly, there is the increase in utility derived from the complete utilization of acquired household specific human capital while the former applies to men and women equally, the latter is a benefit specific to women who have been raised in traditional households that restricted their capital accumulation to household oriented skills. In such cases, the women will have an inevitably larger gain from marriage than men will, and the net difference would be equalized through the payment of an appropriate amount of dowry. Both the "marriage squeeze" theory of excess supply of women in the marriage market as well the theory of divergent patterns of human capital accumulation rationalize. The existence of dowry in Indian society based on one critical factor: traditional Indian social values. In the theory of the "marriage squeeze," population growth has only affected the size of the female cohort in the marriage market because of the social values that compel women to be married by a certain age. In the theory of divergent human capital accumulation, social mandates, such as those that limit the procurement of human capital for daughters to household oriented skills, as well as those that force women to transfer all assets to the family-in-law after marriage, inevitably put many women in situations where they must rely on marriage for economic sustenance. Examined from this perspective, the main evil behind the perpetuation of the dowry tradition lies in the restrictive and frequently detrimental Indian social views on marriage. The effect of dowry on the welfare of Indian society, however, is further complicated by certain social ills that are inextricably linked with the tradition. Such effects, which include dowry related violence and abuse, bride burning, wife murder, and female infanticide, constitute some of the most highly detrimental ills perpetrated against Indian women. Effects of Dowry the provisions and acts against dowry in the Indian legal code are largely ineffective. The phenomenon is too pervasive and too prevalent in rural communities (where civil law is hardly understood let alone observed) to be influenced by basically any kind of legal statutes. Moreover, studies have shown that a majority of police and other security officials regard dowry as a family issue in which the law, the government, or the police should not interfere As such, the expected punishment for violating legal codes regarding dowry is practically zero, and families continue to practice the giving of dowry according to tradition. Furthermore, the ineffectiveness of the legal codes also means that the dowry is essentially irrecoverable upon termination of the marriage. The lack of legal enforcement of laws pertaining to the family results in a depressing but economically legitimate rational for the perpetration of two very serious social ills: wife murder and female infanticide. Dowry-related Wife Abuse and Murder Because of the practically nonexistent expected punishment for legal violations concerning dowry and because men in Indian society do not generally face any negative economic or societal consequences upon dissolution of a marriage, the existence of dowry in effect induces a man to eliminate his current wife if the expected gains from doing so exceed the gains from continuing to be with her. Essentially, a man who can gain more from the potential dowry of a second marriage than from the benefits of remaining with his first wife is more likely to murder his current wife, especially if there is a low probability of conviction. In a similar vein, wife abuse may be used as a means of inducing a woman to leave a marriage, thereby allowing the husband to contract a second marriage and appropriate a second dowry without the legal risk (however small) of committing murder. Although this economic rational has yet to be adequately substantiated through empirical research, the argument is convincing particularly in light of the incredible pervasiveness of dowry-related wife abuse and murder. Incidents of violence and murders of wives due to issues of dowry first began to be reported in the early 1980's. Stories emerged of women who were burned to death, beaten and abused, murdered, and who committed suicide because of families-in-law who relentless harassed brides on issues related to insufficient dowry. By 1994, the Home Ministry's National Crime Record Bureau clocked a 'dowry death' at every moment. In a country where people rarely report acts of domestic violence, however, even these grossly disturbing figures likely represent only a fraction of the actual dowry deaths that took place during these years These horrific episodes of violence and murder can be seen as the combined result of an inadequately enforced legal system along with an age-old tradition that inherently undermines the relative economic self-sufficiency of women. Female Infanticide In a similar vein, the dowry system may be seen as partly responsible for the female infanticide that occurs all over rural India. Because of the same lack of legal enforcement that has exacerbated dowry-related abuse and murder, the phenomenon of female infanticide is prevalent among Indian families (particularly in rural communities) where the additional cost of dowry for a third or fourth daughter may greatly exceed the family's financial capacity. Again, economic empirical work has yet to explore this correlation, but the raw data and prevalent attitudes are staggering. Government employed midwives revealed in interviews that they "feared for a newborn's life if it was so unfortunate as to be the third or fourth girl born into a poor family of farm laborers...such a family could not possibly afford the price of another girl's dowry...'putting the child to sleep'...seemed their only choice Both dowry-related murders as well as female infanticide are unfortunate and highly deleterious symptoms of India's dowry system. Imposing a highly negative impact on the social welfare of women in Indian society, these phenomena must be addressed as what they are—symptoms of a more significant root problem: that is, the prevailing social and cultural ideology that led to the existence of dowry in the first place. Conclusion Elimination of dowry and of the negative impact it impresses on Indian social welfare requires a twofold system of policies. Firstly, the domestic violence, murder, and female infanticide that result from the dowry tradition must be abolished through increased enforcement of legal provisions such as those in the Dowry Prohibition Act of 1961. By vehemently prosecuting and convicting perpetrators of dowry violence, the expected punishment could be increased enough to offset the benefits of committing such dowry related crime, thereby reducing the overall frequency of occurrence. Secondly, given that crimes related to dowry are rooted in dominant Indian social, religious, and ideological forces, the complete eradication of dowry can only be attained when these social and religious attitudes are forced to change. It has been examined in this paper that the two primary causes of dowry are the excess supply of women in the Indian marriage market and the systematic under-accumulation of market specific human capital by women that causes a discrepancy in marital gains for men and women. In order to stop the perpetuation of the dowry tradition and its associated social ills, the relative gains from marriage for men and women must first be equalized. This can only be accomplished through a fundamental shift in Indian social attitudes about both marriage and women. Perceptions about appropriate roles for women must evolve to include education and employment, the current requirement that brides surrender all future assets to in-laws must be changed so that parents can depend on daughters as well as sons in their old age, and finally, the government must undertake sustained action to prevent employment and wage discrimination against women in the labor market. Unfortunately, there is an enormous period of lag time between the time when calls for social change are actually made and the time when societal beliefs and customs actually begin to transform. Today, dowry continues to be a socially accepted and rational outcome of the current Indian marriage market. True progress in the elimination of the dowry system will only come through endeavors to create awareness among Indian communities about the negative effects of dowry, through programs and government sanctions that endorse education and employment for women of all ages, and through a fundamental change in the attitudes of Indian peoples.